Time
book

illustrated by Jane Bottomley

MACDONALD

It's morning! Time to get up.

Today there's lots to do.

Breakfast has to be fast.
Mum's late for work.

Kate's school starts in half an hour.
William and Dad will take her there.

Yesterday the postman was late.

Today he is early.

William and Dad have work to do.
They want to finish it before lunch.

After lunch they go shopping.

They buy food for tonight's dinner.

When Kate comes home from school,
it's tea-time.

Mum and Dad are getting dinner ready.
William will go to bed soon.

Now it's time to go to sleep.
But first, William and Mum read a story.

Tomorrow, William and Dad will go to the park.